General Instructions

Choose the right yarn . . .

We made our models in Spinrite® Berella® Country Garden D.K., 100% wool or Patons Look At Me! but you can use any similar yarn in sport or DK weight.

We know you hate the word "gauge" . . .

But if you don't take time to check your gauge, the sock will not fit. All the socks are knitted to a stitch gauge of 7 sts = 1" when worked in stockinette stitch (knit 1 row, purl 1 row). But at least you don't have to worry about row gauge when knitting socks!

We suggest a Size 4 needle — but you should use whatever size gives you the specified gauge.

Round and round we go . . .

Our baby socks are knitted on a set of four double-point needles. This avoids sewn seams and makes the foot more comfortable to wear.

When working with four needles in the round, the stitches are divided onto three needles, and the fourth is used to make the stitches (**Fig 1**).

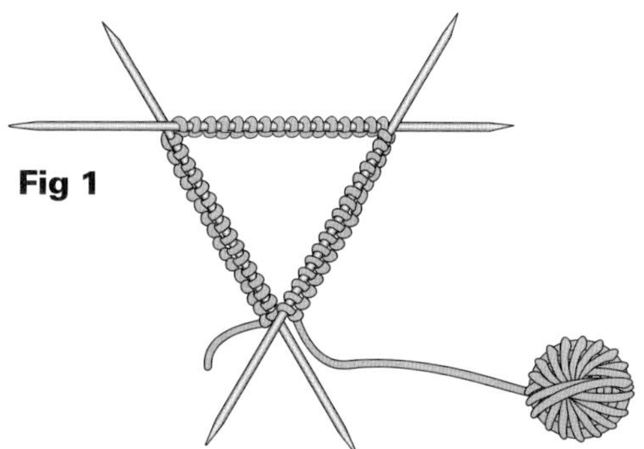

Fig 1

Cast on for elasticity . . .

A beautiful hand-knitted sock doesn't do the wearer much good if the cast-on edge of the cuff is too tight to go over the foot! So since all of our socks are worked from the cuff down, you need to use a cast-on method that gives a lot of stretch. This is the method we used for our socks:

All necessary stitches are cast onto one needle, then separated onto three needles as instructed in the patterns.

To begin, make a slip knot and place the loop on the needle in your right hand, leaving a long strand. For these socks you will need a 36" strand end.

Step 1:

Place the thumb and index finger of your left hand between the long strand and the strand coming from the skein of yarn; close your other three fingers over the strands to hold them against your palm. Spread your thumb and index fingers apart and draw the yarn into a V **(Fig 2)**.

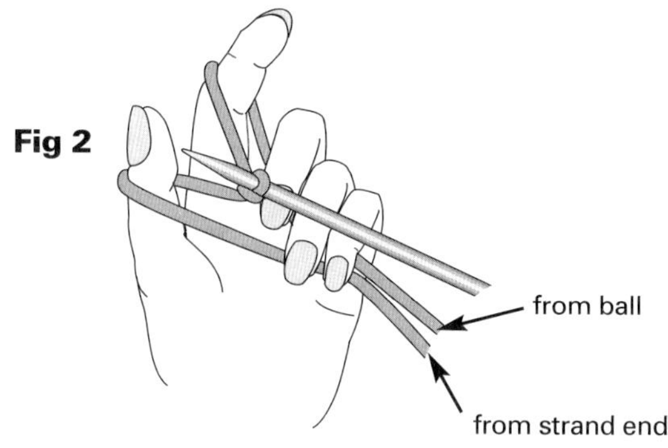

Fig 2

Step 2:

Place the needle in front of the strand around your thumb and bring it underneath this strand; carry needle over and under the strand on your index finger **(Fig 3)**; draw through loop on thumb **(Fig 4)**.

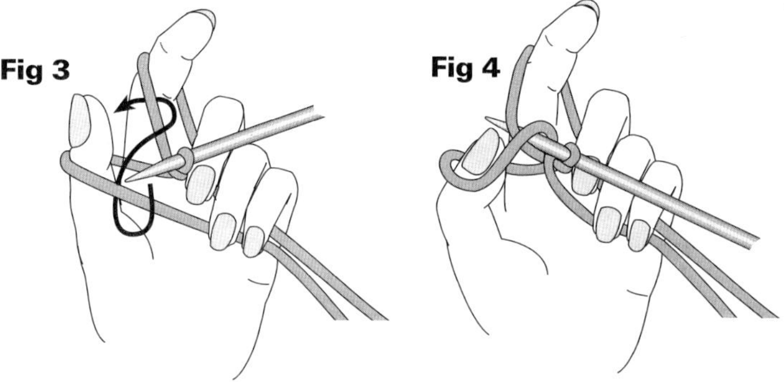

Fig 3 Fig 4

Step 3:

Drop the loop from your thumb and draw up the strand to form a stitch on the needle.

Repeat Steps 1 through 3 until you have cast on the number of stitches indicated in the pattern. Remember to count the beginning slip knot as a stitch.

Hint: Your cast-on stitches must be loose so the sock will stretch when pulled over your foot. The stitches should move easily on the needle. If you tend to cast on tightly, use a larger size needle, or cast on using two needles held together.

continued

Knitting with four needles . . .

On the first row, join the work divided on the three needles by inserting the fourth **(free)** needle into the first stitch on the first needle **(Fig 5)**. When the stitches on Needle 1 are worked, use the now free needle to work the stitches on the next needle; repeat on the third needle. **Hint:** To avoid gaps between needles, pull yarn tightly across to the first stitch of each new needle.

Fig 5

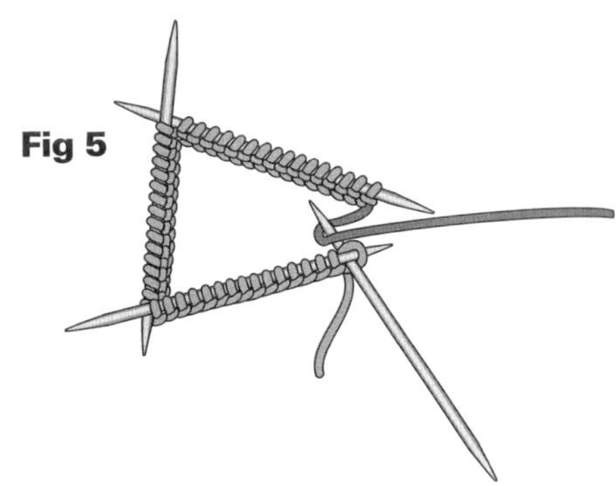

Anatomy of a sock . . .

Fig 6

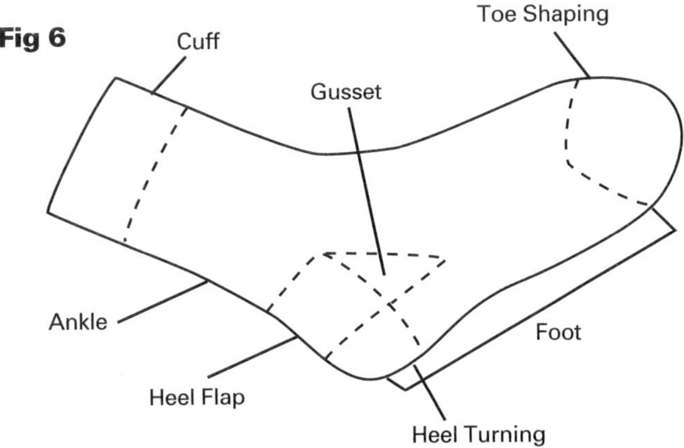

Turning the heel . . .

Since a foot is at an angle to the leg, socks must be shaped the same way. To do this, we use a series of decrease rows after the heel flap is worked to change the direction of the work. This is fun to do, and is called turning a heel.

For example:

If you are working with 32 stitches, place 16 stitches on the needle and 16 stitches on a stitch holder. These stitches on the stitch holder are left unworked while a heel flap is worked on the 16 stitches. Work straight for the number of inches specified in the pattern.

Then work 3 decrease rows. You have 10 stitches on the needle. Turning the heel has been completed.

Picking up stitches . . .

After turning the heel in a sock pattern, it is necessary to pick up stitches along both sides of the heel flap. When working with sport weight yarn, picking up stitches is best done with a size F (3.75mm) crochet hook, then slipping the stitches from it to the knitting needle. (A knitting needle may be used instead of the crochet hook.)

To pick up a stitch, hold the knitting with its right side facing you. Hold yarn from the skein in your left hand, behind the work, and hold the crochet hook in your right hand. Insert hook into work from front to back, one stitch (no more than 2 threads) from the edge **(Fig 7)**; hook yarn and pull a loop back through work, making one stitch on hook **(Fig 8)**.

Fig 7

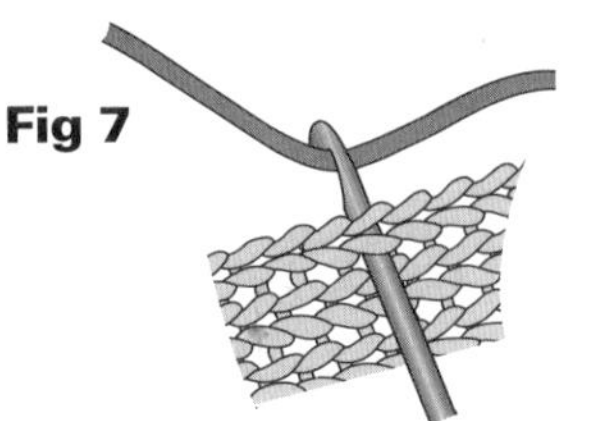

Fig 8

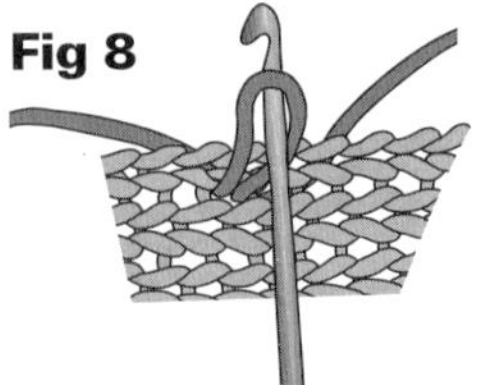

Now slip stitch off crochet hook and onto knitting needle, being sure to have the stitch in the correct position, without twisting it **(Fig 9)**.

Fig 9

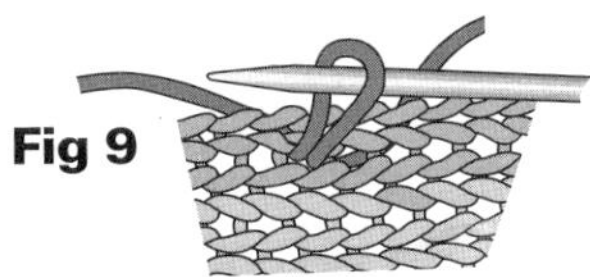

The specific pattern will indicate the exact number of stitches to pick up along each side of the heel flap.

Special Techniques

Weaving on Two Needles—Kitchener Stitch . . .

This method of weaving is used for the toes of the socks.

To weave the edges together and form an unbroken line of stockinette stitch, divide all stitches evenly onto two knitting needles - one behind the other.

Thread yarn into tapestry needle; with wrong sides together, work from right to left as follows:

Step 1:
Insert tapestry needle into the first stitch on the front needle as to purl **(Fig 1)**. Draw yarn through stitch, leaving stitch on knitting needle.

Fig 1

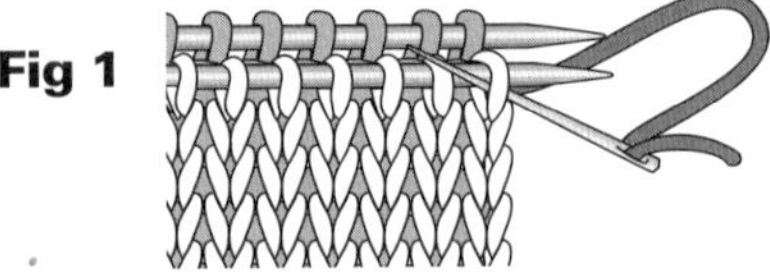

Step 2:
Insert tapestry needle into the first stitch on the back needle as to purl **(Fig 2)**. Draw yarn through stitch and slip stitch off knitting needle.

Fig 2

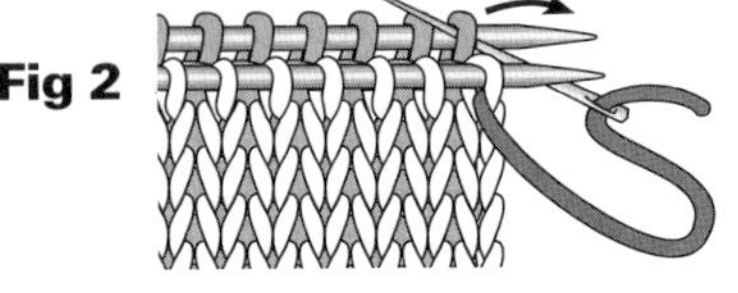

Step 3:
Insert tapestry needle into the next stitch on same **(back)** needle as to knit **(Fig 3)**, leaving stitch on knitting needle.

Fig 3
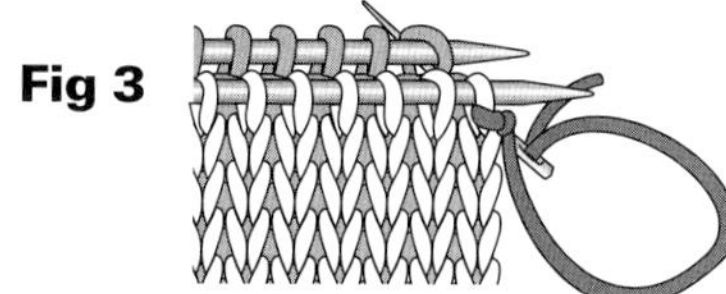

Step 4:
Insert tapestry needle into the first stitch on the front needle as to knit **(Fig 4)**. Draw yarn through stitch and slip stitch off knitting needle.

Fig 4
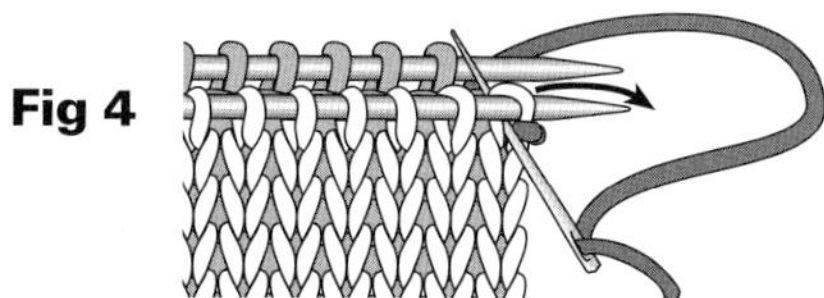

Step 5:
Insert tapestry needle into the next stitch on same **(front)** needle as to purl **(Fig 5)**. Draw yarn through stitch, leaving stitch on knitting needle.

Fig 5
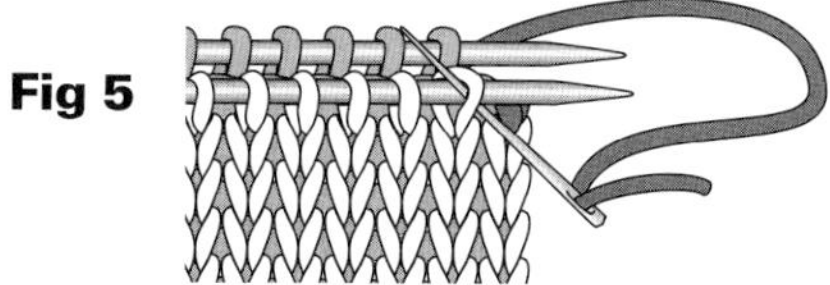

Repeat Steps 2 through 5 until one stitch is left on each needle. Then repeat Steps 2 through 4. Finish off.

Hint: When weaving, do not pull yarn tightly or too loosely; woven stitches should be the same size as adjacent knitted stitches.

Working with charts . . .

The charts in this book are used when knitting with more than one color per row or round.

When working in rows, read odd numbered rows from right to left, and even numbered rows from left to right.

Odd numbered rows represent the right side of your work, and are usually knit. Even numbered rows represent the wrong side of your work, and are usually purled.

When working in rounds, every row on the chart is a right side row, and are always read from right to left.

Abbreviations and Symbols

beg . . . . . begin(ning)
bl(s) . . . . . back loop(s)
gm(s) . . . . . gram(s)
inc . . . . . increase
K. . . . . . knit
oz . . . . . ounce(s)
P . . . . . purl
patt . . . . . pattern
PSSO . . . . . pass slipped st over
rem . . . . . remain(ing)
rep . . . . . repeat(ing)
rnd(s) . . . . . round(s)
sk. . . . . . skip
sl . . . . . slip
sl st(s) . . . . . slip stitch(es)
SSK. . . . . . slip, slip, knit
st(s) . . . . . stitch(es)
tog. . . . . . together
yb . . . . . yarn back
yd(s). . . . . . yard(s)
yf . . . . . yarn forward
YO . . . . . yarn over

***** An asterisk is used to mark the beginning of a portion of instructions which will be worked more than once; thus, "rep from ***** twice more" means after working the instructions once, repeat the instructions following the asterisk twice more (3 times in all).

—The number after a long dash at the end of a row or round indicates the number of stitches you should have when the row or round has been completed.

( ) Parentheses are used to enclose instructions which should be worked the exact number of times specified immediately following the parentheses, such as (K2, P2) twice. They are also used to provide additional information to clarify instructions.

Basic Sock

Sizes:
6-12 months (18-24 months)

Foot length:
$3^{3}/_{4}$" ($4^{1}/_{4}$")
Note: Instructions are written for Size 6-12 months; changes for larger size are in parentheses.

Materials (sufficient yarn for both sizes)**:**
Sport weight yarn, $1^{3}/_{4}$ oz (152 yds, 50 gms) variegated
Note: Our photographed sock was made with Patons Look At Me!, Happy Days #6376.
Size 3 (3.25mm) double-pointed knitting needles, or size required for gauge
Size F (3.75mm) crochet hook (optional for picking up stitches)
Stitch marker
Small stitch holder
Size 18 tapestry needle

Gauge:
In stockinette stitch (knit one row, purl one row):
7 sts = 1"

Special Abbreviation

Slip, Slip, Knit (SSK)**:**
Slip next 2 sts, one at a time, as to knit; insert left-hand needle through both sts from right to left; K2 tog—SSK made.

Instructions

Sock (make 2)
Loosely cast on 32 sts onto one needle. Divide onto 3 needles, having 10 sts on first needle, 12 sts on second needle, and 10 sts on third needle. Mark beg of each rnd.

Cuff:
Rnd 1:
* K1, P1; rep from * around.

Rep Rnd 1 until cuff measures $2^{1}/_{4}$" ($2^{1}/_{2}$").

Next 2 Rnds:
Knit.

Heel:
Slip last 8 sts worked onto free needle; knit first 8 sts of last rnd worked onto same needle (these sts make the heel flap); slip remaining 16 sts onto stitch holder for instep. Turn.

HEEL FLAP:
Note: Heel flap is worked in rows.

Row 1 (wrong side)**:**
Sl 1 as to purl, purl across. Turn.

Row 2 (right side)**:**
Sl 1 as to knit, knit across row. Turn.

Rows 3 through 16:
Rep Rows 1 and 2 seven times more.

Turning Heel:
Row 1 (wrong side)**:**
P10, P2 tog; P1. Turn, leaving rem 3 sts unworked.

Row 2 (right side)**:**
Sl 1 as to knit, K5, SSK (see Special Abbreviation); K1. Turn, leaving rem 3 sts unworked.

Row 3:
Sl 1 as to purl, P6, P2 tog; P1. Turn, leaving rem st unworked.

Row 4:
Sl 1 as to knit, K7, SSK; K1. Turn, leaving rem st unworked.

Row 5:
Sl 1 as to purl, P8, P2 tog—10 sts. Turn.

Row 6:
Sl 1 as to knit, K8, SSK—10 sts. Do not turn.

Gusset:
With right side facing you and one free needle, pick up 8 sts along left-hand side of heel flap; on next free needle, K16 sts from stitch holder; on last free needle, pick up 8 sts along right-hand side of heel flap; knit first 5 sts of heel onto same needle; slip rem 5 sts of heel onto beg of first needle—42 sts.

Rnd 1:
On first needle, knit to last 3 sts; K2 tog; K1; on second needle, knit across; on third needle, K1, SSK; knit rem sts—40 sts.

Rnd 2:
Knit.

Rnds 3 through 10:
Rep Rnds 1 and 2 four times more. At end of Rnd 10—32 sts.

Foot:
Rnd 1:
Knit.

Rep Rnd 1 until foot measures 2¾" (3¼").

Toe Shaping:
Rnd 1:
On first needle, knit to last 3 sts; K2 tog; K1; on second needle, K1, SSK; knit to last 3 sts; K2 tog; K1; on third needle, K1, SSK; knit rem sts—28 sts.

Rnd 2:
Knit.

Rnds 3 through 8:
Rep Rnds 1 and 2 three times more. At end of Rnd 8—16 sts.

Rnd 9:
Rep Rnd 1. At end of rnd—12 sts.

Knit sts from first needle onto third needle.

Cut yarn, leaving a 12" end for weaving.

Finishing

With tapestry needle and end, weave toe together (see Special Techniques beginning on page 2). Weave in all ends.

Stripes & Checks

Sizes:
6-12 months (18-24 months)

Foot length:
3¾" (4¼")

Note: Instructions are written for Size 6-12 months; changes for larger size are in parentheses.

Materials (sufficient yarn for both sizes)**:**
Sport weight yarn, 1 oz (77 yds, 29 gms) each, blue, orange, and yellow
Note: Our photographed sock was made with Patons Look At Me!, Mid Blue #6359, Mango #6356, and Sunny Yellow #6366.
Size 3 (3.25mm) double-pointed knitting needles, or size required for gauge
Size F (3.75mm) crochet hook (optional for picking up stitches)
Stitch marker
Small stitch holder
Size 18 tapestry needle

Gauge:
In stockinette stitch (knit one row, purl one row)
7 sts = 1"

Special Abbreviation

Slip, Slip, Knit (SSK)**:**
Slip next 2 sts, one at a time, as to knit; insert left-hand needle through both sts from right to left; K2 tog—SSK made.

Instructions

Sock (make 2)
With blue, loosely cast on 32 sts onto one needle. Divide onto 3 needles, having 10 sts on first needle, 12 sts on second needle, and 10 sts on third needle. Mark beg of each rnd.

continued

Cuff:

Rnd 1:
* K2, P2; rep from * around.

Rnds 2 through 8:
Rep Rnd 1.

Ankle:

Note: When working with more than one color in the same rnd, carry unused strand loosely on wrong side of work. Bring new color under old color to prevent holes in work.

Rnd 1:
* With blue, K2; with orange, K2; rep from * 7 times more.

Rnd 2:
Rep Rnd 1.

Rnd 3:
* With yellow, K2; with blue, K2; rep from * 7 times more.

Rnd 4:
Rep Rnd 3.

Rnds 5 through 12:
Rep Rnds 1 through 4 twice more.

Slip last 8 sts worked onto free needle; with blue, knit first 8 sts of last rnd onto same needle; slip rem16 sts onto stitch holder for instep. Turn.

Heel:

Row 1 (wrong side**):**
With blue, sl 1 as to purl, purl across. Turn.

Row 2 (right side**):**
With orange, sl 1 as to knit, knit across. Turn.

Row 3:
With orange, sl 1 as to purl, purl across. Turn.

Row 4:
With blue, sl 1 as to knit, knit across. Turn.

Row 5:
With blue, sl 1 as to purl, purl across. Turn.

Row 6:
With yellow, sl 1 as to knit, knit across. Turn.

Row 7:
With yellow, sl 1 as to purl, purl across. Turn.

Rows 8 and 9:
Rep Rows 4 and 5.

Rows 10 and 11:
Rep Rows 2 and 3.

Rows 12 and 13:
Rep Rows 4 and 5.

Row 14:
Rep Row 4.

Turning Heel:

Row 1 (wrong side**):**
With blue, P10, P2 tog; P1. Turn, leaving rem 3 sts unworked.

Row 2 (right side**):**
Sl 1 as to knit, K5, SSK **(**see Special Abbreviation**)**; K1. Turn, leaving rem 3 sts unworked.

Row 3:
Sl 1 as to purl, P6, P2 tog; P1. Turn, leaving rem st unworked.

Row 4:
Sl 1 as to knit, K7, SSK; K1. Turn, leaving rem st unworked.

Row 5:
Sl 1 as to purl, P8, P2 tog—10 sts. Turn.

Row 6:
Sl 1 as to knit, K8, SSK—10 sts. Do not turn.

Gusset:
With right side facing you and one free needle, with blue, pick up 8 sts along left-hand side of heel flap; on next free needle, K16 sts from stitch holder; on last free needle, pick up 8 sts along right-hand side of heel flap; knit first 5 sts of heel onto same needle; slip rem 5 sts of heel onto beg of first needle—42 sts.

Rnd 1:
On first needle, knit to last 3 sts; K2 tog; K1; on second needle, knit across; on third needle, K1, SSK; knit rem sts—40 sts.

Rnd 2:
With orange, knit.

Rnd 3:
With orange, rep Rnd 1.

Rnds 4 and 5:
With blue, rep Rnds 2 and 3.

Rnds 6 and 7:
With yellow, rep Rnds 2 and 3.

Rnds 8 and 9:
With blue, rep Rnds 2 and 3. At end of Rnd 9—32 sts.

Foot:
Continuing in stripe patt, knit every rnd until foot measures about 2$^{3}/_{4}$" **(**3$^{1}/_{4}$"**)**, and you have completed 2 rnds of last color.

Toe Shaping:

Rnd 1:
With blue, on first needle, knit to last 3 sts, K2 tog; K1; on second needle, K1, SSK; knit to last 3 sts, K2 tog; K1; on third needle, K1, SSK; knit rem sts—28 sts.

Rnd 2:
Knit.

Rnds 3 through 8:
Rep Rnds 1 and 2 three times more. At end of Rnd 8—16 sts.

Rnd 9:
Rep Rnd 1. At end of rnd—12 sts.

Knit sts from first needle onto third needle.

Cut yarn, leaving a 12" end for weaving.

Finishing
With tapestry needle and end, weave toe together **(**see Special Techniques beginning on page 2**)**. Weave in all ends.

Sweet Heart

Back of heel features a heart motif

Sizes:
6-12 months (18-24 months)

Foot length:
$3^3/_4$" ($4^1/_4$")

Note: Instructions are written for Size 6-12 months; changes for larger size are in parentheses.

Materials (sufficient yarn for both sizes**):**
Sport weight yarn, 1 oz (77 yds, 29 gms) each, red and off white

Note: Our photographed sock was made with Berella® Country Garden D.K., Brick Red #22, and Snowdrop #01.

Size 3 (3.25mm) double-pointed knitting needles, or size required for gauge

Size F (3.75mm) crochet hook (optional for picking up stitches)

Stitch marker

One small bobbin

Small stitch holder

Size 18 tapestry needle

Gauge:
In stockinette stitch (knit one row, purl one row):
7 sts = 1"

Special Abbreviation

Slip, Slip, Knit (SSK):
Slip next 2 sts, one at a time, as to knit; insert left-hand needle through both sts from right to left; K2 tog—SSK made.

Instructions

Note: Wind bobbin with red. Set aside.

Sock (make 2)
With red, loosely cast on 32 sts onto one needle. Divide onto 3 needles, having 10 sts on first needle, 12 sts on second needle, and 10 sts on third needle. Mark beg of each rnd.

Cuff:

Rnd 1:
* K1, P1; rep from * around.

Rep Rnd 1 until cuff measures 2".

Ankle:

Note: When working with more than one color in the same rnd, carry unused strand loosely on wrong side of work. Bring new color under old color to prevent holes in work.

Rnds 1 and 2:
Knit.

Rnd 3:
* With off white, K1; with red, K1; rep from * around.

Rnd 4:
* With red, K1; with off white, K1; rep from * around.

Rnds 5 and 6:
With red, knit.

Heel:

Note: Heel is worked back and forth in rows. When working from **Chart A**, work wrong-side rows from left to right and right-side rows from right to left. Do not carry white beyond Row 3; join red bobbin on Row 4 when needed.

Chart A

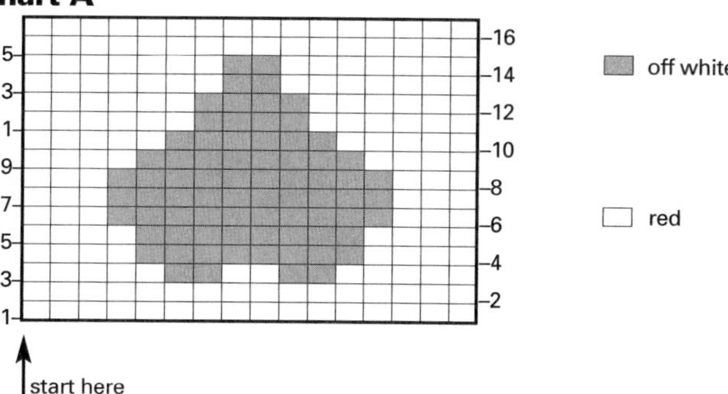

Slip last 8 sts worked onto free needle; knit first 8 sts from first needle onto same needle; slip rem 16 sts onto stitch holder for instep. Turn.

Row 1 (wrong side)**:**
With red, sl 1 as to purl, purl across.

Row 2 (right side)**:**
Sl 1 as to knit, knit across.

Rows 3 through 16:
Continue in stockinette st, slipping first st of each row, and following Rows 3 through 16 of Chart A for color changes.

Turning Heel, Gusset, and Foot:
With red, work same as for Basic Sock on page 4.

With off white, knit one rnd.

Toe Shaping and Finishing:
With off white, work same as for Basic Sock on page 5.

Tiny Cables

Sizes:
6-12 months (18-24 months)

Foot length:
3³/₄" (4¹/₄")

Note: Instructions are written for Size 6-12 months; changes for larger size are in parentheses.

Materials (sufficient yarn for both sizes)**:**
Sport weight yarn, 1³/₄ oz (135 yds, 50 gms) violet
Note: Our photographed sock was made with Berella® Country Garden D.K., Wild Violet #28.
Size 3 (3.25mm) double-pointed knitting needles, or size required for gauge
Size F (3.75mm) crochet hook (optional for picking up stitches)
Stitch marker
Small stitch holder
Size 18 tapestry needle

Gauge:
In stockinette stitch (knit one row, purl one row):
7 sts = 1"

Special Abbreviation

Slip, Slip, Knit (SSK)**:**
Slip next 2 sts, one at a time, as to knit; insert left-hand needle through both sts from right to left; K2 tog—SSK made.

Instructions

Sock (make 2)
Loosely cast on 30 sts onto one needle. Divide onto 3 needles, having 10 sts on each needle. Mark beg of each rnd.

Cuff:
Rnd 1:
* K3, P2; rep from * around.

Rnd 2:
Rep Rnd 1.

Rnd 3:
* Sl 1 as to knit, K2 tog, PSSO; P2; rep from * around—18 sts.

Rnd 4:
* In next st work (K1, P1, K1); P2; rep from * around—30 sts.

Rep Rnds 1 through 4 until piece measures 2¹/₄" (2¹/₂") from cast-on edge, ending by working a Rnd 1.

Next Rnd:
* Inc (knit in front and back of next st); K14; rep from * once more—32 sts.

Heel, Gusset, Foot, Toe Shaping, and Finishing:
Work same as for Basic Sock beginning on page 4.

Spring Stripes

Sizes:
6-12 months (18-24 months)

Foot length:
3¾" (4¼")

Note: Instructions are written for Size 6-12 months; changes for larger size are in parentheses.

Materials (sufficient yarn for both sizes)**:**
Sport weight yarn, 1 oz (77 yds, 29 gms) each, lt green, white, and pink

Note: Our photographed sock was made with Berella® Country Garden D.K., White Grape #41, Snowdrop #01, and Scallop Pink #17.

Size 3 (3.25mm) double-pointed knitting needles, or size required for gauge
Size F (3.75mm) crochet hook (optional for picking up stitches)
Stitch marker
Small stitch holder
Size 18 tapestry needle

Gauge:
In stockinette stitch (knit one row, purl one row)**:**
7 sts = 1"

Special Abbreviation

Slip, Slip, Knit (SSK)**:**
Slip next 2 sts, one at a time, as to knit; insert left-hand needle through both sts from right to left; K2 tog—SSK made.

Instructions

Sock (make 2)
With lt green, loosely cast on 32 sts onto one needle. Divide onto 3 needles, having 10 sts on first needle, 12 sts on second needle, and 10 sts on third needle. Mark beg of each rnd.

Cuff:

Rnd 1:
* K1, P1; rep from * around.

Rnd 2:
Rep Rnd 1.

Rnd 3:
With white, knit.

Rnd 4:
With white, * K1, P1; rep from * around.

Rnd 5:
With pink, knit.

Rnd 6:
With pink, * K1, P1; rep from * around.

Rnd 7:
With lt green, knit.

Rnd 8:
With lt green, * K1, P1; rep from * around.

Rnds 9 through 14:
Rep Rnds 3 through 8.

Rnds 15 through 18:
Rep Rnds 3 through 6.

Rnds 19 and 20:
With lt green, knit.

Heel:
With lt green, work Heel Flap and Turning Heel same as for Basic Sock on page 4.

Gusset and Foot:
Beg with white, work same as for Basic Sock beginning on page 4, keeping in stripe patt as follows:

2 rnds white

2 rnds pink

2 rnds lt green

Toe Shaping and Finishing:
With next color in stripe sequence, work same as for Basic Sock on page 5.

Denim Blue

Sizes:
6-12 months (18-24 months)

Foot length:
3¾" (4¼")

Note: Instructions are written for Size 6-12 months; changes for larger size are in parentheses.

Materials (sufficient yarn for both sizes)**:**
Sport weight yarn, 1 oz (77 yds, 29 gms) each, med blue and lt blue
Note: Our photographed sock was made with Berella® Country Garden D.K., Delphinium #32 and Bayberry #31.
Size 3 (3.25mm) double-pointed knitting needles, or size required for gauge
Size F (3.75mm) crochet hook (optional for picking up stitches)
Stitch marker
Small stitch holder
Size 18 tapestry needle

Gauge:
In stockinette stitch (knit one row, purl one row):
7 sts = 1"

Special Abbreviation

Slip, Slip, Knit (SSK)**:**
Slip next 2 sts, one at a time, as to knit; insert left-hand needle through both sts from right to left; K2 tog—SSK made.

Instructions

Sock (make 2)
With lt blue, loosely cast on 32 sts onto one needle. Divide onto 3 needles, having 10 sts on first needle, 12 sts on second needle, and 10 sts on third needle. Mark beg of each rnd.

Cuff:

Rnd 1:
* K1, P1; rep from * around.

Rnd 2:
Rep Rnd 1.

Change to med blue; rep Rnd 1 until cuff measures 2¼" (2 ½").

Next 2 Rnds:
Knit.

Heel:
With lt blue, work same as for Basic Sock on page 4.

Gusset and Foot:
With med blue, work same as for Basic Sock beginning on page 4.

With lt blue, knit one rnd.

Toe Shaping and Finishing:
Work same as for Basic Sock on page 5.

Bobble Top

Sizes:
6-12 months (18-24 months)

Foot length:
3¾" (4¼")
Note: Instructions are written for Size 6-12 months; changes for large size are in parentheses.

Materials (sufficient yarn for both sizes):
Sport weight yarn, 1 oz (77 yds, 29 gms) each, blue and pink
Note: Our photographed sock was made with Patons Look At Me!, Mid Blue #6359 and Hot Pink #6357.
Size 3 (3.25mm) double-pointed knitting needles, or size required for gauge
Size F (3.75mm) crochet hook (optional for picking up stitches)
Stitch marker
Small stitch holder
Size 18 tapestry needle

Gauge:
In stockinette stitch (knit one row, purl one row):
7 sts = 1"

Pattern Stitch
Bobble:
In next st work (K1, P1, K1, P1, K1); slip 2nd, 3rd, 4th, and 5th sts over first st one at a time—bobble made.

Special Abbreviation
Slip, Slip, Knit (SSK):
Slip next 2 sts, one at a time, as to knit; insert left-hand needle through both sts from right to left; K2 tog—SSK made.

Instructions

Sock (make 2)
With pink, loosely cast on 32 sts onto one needle. Divide onto 3 needles, having 10 sts on first needle, 12 sts on second needle, and 10 sts on third needle. Mark beg of each rnd.

Cuff:
Rnd 1:
* K1, P1; rep from * around.

Rnd 2:
Rep Rnd 1.

Rnd 3:
With blue, knit.

Rnd 4:
With blue, * K1, P1, bobble (see Pattern Stitch); P1; rep from * 7 times more.

Rnd 5:
With pink, knit.

Rnd 6:
With pink, * K1, P1; rep from * around.

With blue, rep Rnd 6 until piece measures 2¼" (2½").

Next 2 Rnds:
Knit.

Heel, Gusset, and Foot:
With blue, work same as for Basic Sock beginning on page 4.

With pink, knit one rnd.

Toe Shaping and Finishing:
Work same as for Basic Sock on page 5.

Anchors Away

Sizes:
6-12 months (18-24 months)
Foot length:
3¾" (4¼")
Note: Instructions are written for Size 6-12 months; changes for larger size are in parentheses.

Materials (sufficient yarn for both sizes**):**
Sport weight yarn, 1 oz (77 yds, 29 gms) each, blue and off white
Note: Our photographed sock was made with Berella® Country Garden D.K., Lapis #29 and Snowdrop #01.
Size 3 (3.25mm) double-pointed knitting needles, or size required for gauge
Size F (3.75mm) crochet hook (optional for picking up stitches)
Stitch marker
Small stitch holder
Size 18 tapestry needle

Gauge:
In stockinette stitch **(**knit one row, purl one row**)**:
7 sts = 1"

Special Abbreviation

Slip, Slip, Knit (SSK)**:**
Slip next 2 sts, one at a time, as to knit; insert left-hand needle through both sts from right to left; K2 tog—SSK made.

Instructions

Sock (make 2**)**
With off white, loosely cast on 32 sts onto one needle. Divide onto 3 needles, having 10 sts on first needle, 12 sts on second needle, and 10 sts on third needle. Mark beg of each rnd.

Cuff:
Rnd 1:
* K1, P1; rep from * around.

Rep Rnd 1 until cuff measures 1".

Ankle:
Note: When working from a chart in rnds, read every row from right to left. When working with more than one color in the same rnd, carry unused strand loosely on wrong side of work. Bring new color under old color to prevent holes in work.

Rnds 1 through 11:
Working from **Chart A**, knit each rnd.

Chart A

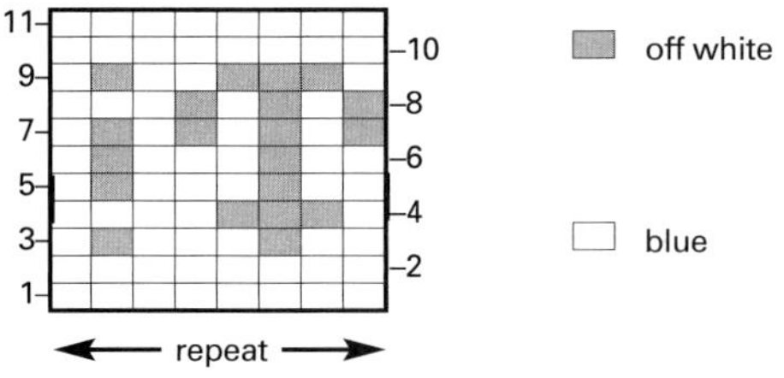

Rnds 12 and 13:
Continuing with blue, knit.

Heel, Gusset, and Foot:
With blue, work same as for Basic Sock beginning on page 4.

With off white, knit one rnd.

Toe Shaping and Finishing:
Work same as for Basic Sock on page 5.

Party-Time Lace

Sizes:
6-12 months (18-24 months)

Foot length:
3¾" (4¼")
Note: Instructions are written for Size 6-12 months; changes for larger size are in parentheses.

Materials (sufficient yarn for both sizes)**:**
Sport weight yarn, 1 3/4 oz (135 yds, 50 gms) pink
Note: Our photographed sock was made with Berella® Country Garden D.K., Heather Pink #24.
Size 3 (3.25mm) double-pointed knitting needles, or size required for gauge
Size F (3.75mm) crochet hook (optional for picking up stitches)
Stitch marker
Small stitch holder
Size 18 tapestry needle

Gauge:
In stockinette stitch (knit one row, purl one row):
7 sts = 1"

Special Abbreviation
Slip, Slip, Knit (SSK)**:**
Slip next 2 sts, one at a time, as to knit; insert left-hand needle through both sts from right to left; K2 tog—SSK made.

Instructions

Sock (make 2)
Loosely cast on 32 sts onto one needle. Divide onto 3 needles, having 10 sts on first needle, 12 sts on second needle, and 10 sts on third needle. Mark beg of each rnd.

Cuff:
Rnd 1:
* K1, P1; rep from * around.

Rep Rnd 1 until cuff measures 1".

Ankle:
Rnds 1 through 3:
Knit.

Rnd 4:
* K5, YO, sl 1 as to knit, K2 tog, PSSO; YO; rep from * around.

Rnd 5:
Knit.

Rnd 6:
* K6, YO, SSK (see Special Abbreviation); rep from * around.

Rnds 7 through 9:
Knit.

Rnd 10:
K1; * YO, sl 1 as to knit, K2 tog, PSSO; YO, K5; rep from * twice more; YO, sl 1 as to knit, K2 tog, PSSO; YO, K4.

Rnd 11:
K2; * YO, SSK; K6; rep from * twice more; YO, SSK; K4.

Rnds 12 and 13:
Knit.

Heel, Gusset, Foot, Toe Shaping and Finishing:
Work same as for Basic Sock beginning on page 4.

Pink Posies

Sizes:
6-12 months (18-24 months)

Foot length:
$3^3/_4$" ($4^1/_4$")

Note: Instructions are written for Size 6-12 months; changes for larger size are in parentheses.

Materials (sufficient yarn for both sizes)**:**
Sport weight yarn, $1^3/_4$ oz (135 yds, 50 gms) white;
5 yds each, pink and green

Note: Our photographed sock was made with Berella® Country Garden D.K., Snowdrop #01, Field Flower #19, and Whaler Blue #35 .

Size 3 (3.25mm) double-pointed knitting needles, or size required for gauge
Size F (3.75mm) crochet hook (optional for picking up stitches)
Stitch marker
Small stitch holder
Size 18 tapestry needle

Gauge:
In stockinette stitch (knit one row, purl one row):
7 sts = 1"

Special Abbreviation

Slip, Slip, Knit (SSK)**:**
Slip next 2 sts, one at a time, as to knit; insert left-hand needle through both sts from right to left; K2 tog—SSK made.

Instructions

Sock (make 2)
With white, loosely cast on 32 sts onto one needle. Divide onto 3 needles, having 10 sts on first needle, 12 sts on second needle, and 10 sts on third needle. Mark beg of each rnd.

Cuff:
Rnd 1:
* K1, P1; rep from * around.

Rep Rnd 1 until cuff measures 1".

Ankle:
Rnd 1:
Knit.

Rep Rnd 1 until piece measures $2^1/_4$" **(**3"**)**.

Heel, Gusset, Foot, and Toe Shaping:
Work same as for Basic Sock beginning on page 4.

Finishing
Step 1:
With tapestry needle and end, weave toe together **(**see Special Techniques beginning on page 2**)**. Weave in all ends.

Step 2:
Referring to photo for placement, with pink, stitch 4 flowers evenly spaced around ankle of sock using 2 bouillion stitches for each rose **(**see instructions below**)**. With green, add 2 stitches under each flower for stems and 2 leaves using lazy daisy stitch **(**see instructions below**)**.

Bullion Stitch
Thread tapestry needle with yarn. Bring yarn up at 1 and pull thread through. Stitch down at 2 **(a)** and come up again at 1; do not pull needle completely through. Wrap working yarn around top of needle 6 to 8 times **(b)**. Pull needle through in direction shown by arrow **(c)** with non-stitching hand, while gently holding twist closely around needle with stitching hand. Stitch down at 2 **(d)**, pulling firmly to shape stitch.

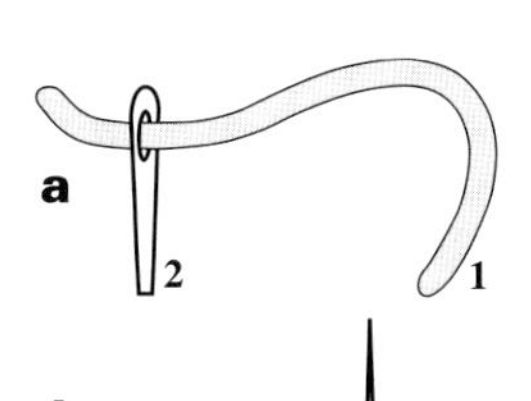

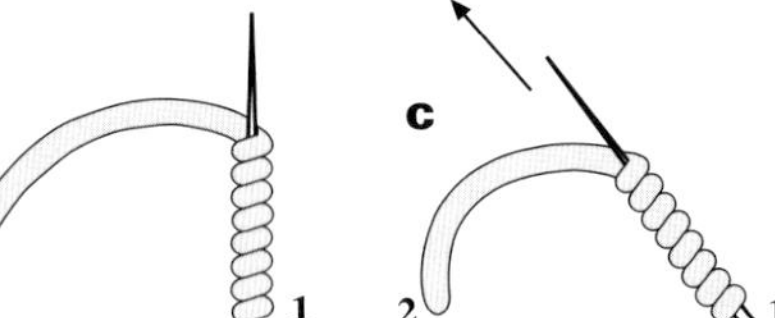

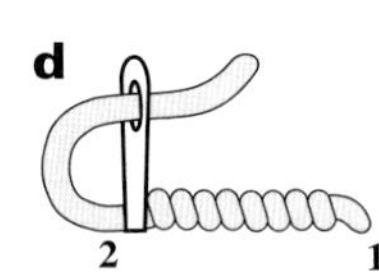

Lazy Daisy Stitch
Thread tapestry needle with yarn. Bring yarn up (1), loop yarn, insert needle in same space (2), and bring up at loop end (3). Pull needle through, adjust loop, and take a small stitch down over loop to secure (4).

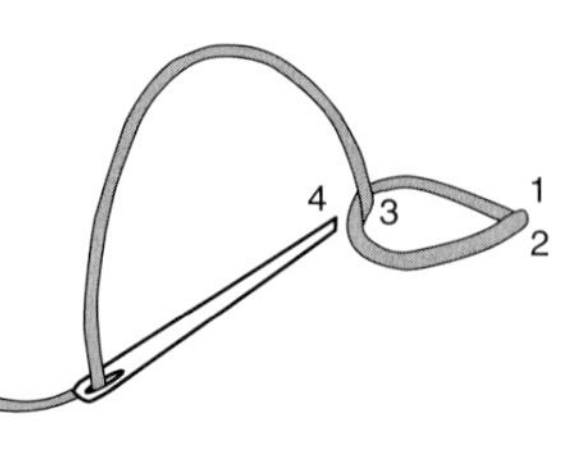

Future MBA

Sizes:
6-12 months (18-24 months)

Foot length:
3¾" (4¼")

Note: Instructions are written for Size 6-12 months; changes for larger size are in parentheses.

Materials (sufficient yarn for both sizes)**:**
Sport weight yarn, 1 oz (77 yds, 29 gms) each, white and black; 5 yds red
Note: Our photographed sock was made with Berella® Country Garden D.K., Snowdrop #01, Black #64, and Brick Red #33.
Size 3 (3.25mm) double-pointed knitting needles, or size required for gauge
Size F (3.75mm) crochet hook (optional for picking up stitches)
Stitch marker
Small stitch holder
Size 18 tapestry needle

Gauge:
In stockinette stitch (knit one row, purl one row):
7 sts = 1"

Special Abbreviation

Slip, Slip, Knit (SSK)**:**
Slip next 2 sts, one at a time, as to knit; insert left-hand needle through both sts from right to left; K2 tog—SSK made.

Instructions

Sock (make 2)
With black, loosely cast on 32 sts onto one needle. Divide onto 3 needles, having 10 sts on first needle, 12 sts on second needle, and 10 sts on third needle. Mark beg of each rnd.

Cuff:

Rnd 1:
* K1, P1; rep from * around.

Rnds 2 through 7 (8):
Rep Rnd 1.

Rnd 8 (9):
* K7, inc (knit in front and back of next st); rep from * 3 times more—36 sts.

Ankle:
Note: When working from chart, read each rnd from right to left. When working with more than one color in the same rnd, carry unused strand loosely on wrong side of work. Bring new color under old color to prevent holes in work.

Rnds 1 through 8 (12):
With white, black, and red, work from **Chart A**.

Chart A

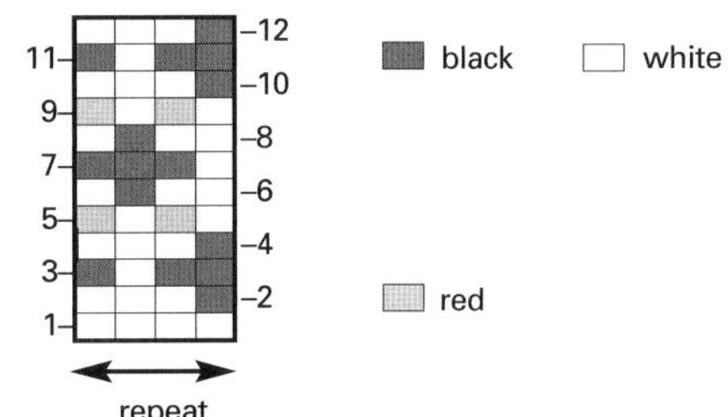

Rnd 9 (13):
With white, * K7, K2 tog; rep from * 3 times more—32 sts.

Heel:
Note: Heel is worked back and forth in rows.

Slip last 8 sts of last rnd worked onto free needle; knit next 8 sts of next rnd onto same needle; slip rem 16 sts onto stitch holder for instep. Turn.

Row 1 (wrong side)**:**
With black, purl. Turn.

Row 2 (right side)**:**
Sl 1 as to knit, knit across. Turn.

Row 3:
Sl 1 as to purl, purl across. Turn.

Rows 4 through 13:
Rep Rows 2 and 3 six times.

Row 14:
Rep Row 2.

TURNING HEEL:
Work heel turning same as for Basic Sock on page 4.

Gusset and Foot:
With white, work same as for Basic Sock beginning on page 4.

With black, knit one row.

Toe Shaping and Finishing:
Work same as for basic sock on page 5.

Circus Fun

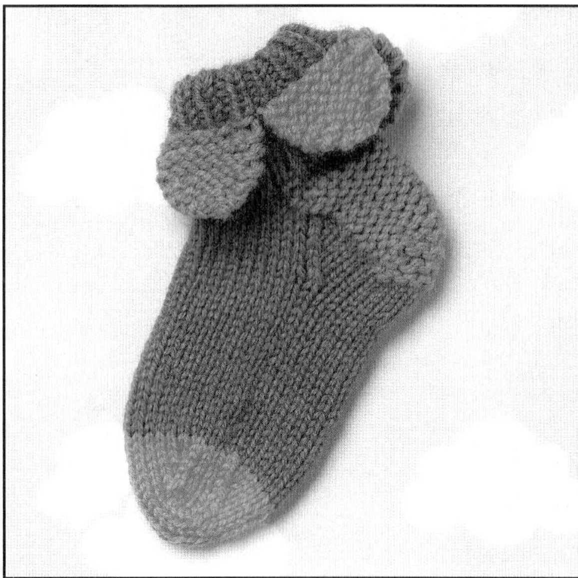

Sizes:
6-12 months (18-24 months)

Foot length:
3³/₄" (4¹/₄")

Note: Instructions are written for Size 6-12 months; changes for larger size are in parentheses.

Materials (sufficient yarn for both sizes**):**
Sport weight yarn, 1³/₄ oz (152 yds, 50 gms) blue;
5 yds each, orange and green
Note: Our photographed sock was made with Patons Look At Me!, Cornflower Blue #6382 , Orange #6385 and Jade #6363.
Size 3 (3.25mm) double-pointed knitting needles, or size required for gauge
Size F (3.75mm) crochet hook (optional for picking up stitches)
Stitch marker
Three small stitch holders
Size 18 tapestry needle

Gauge:
In stockinette stitch **(**knit one row, purl one row**)**:
7 sts = 1"

Special Abbreviation

Slip, Slip, Knit (SSK)**:**
Slip next 2 sts, one at a time, as to knit; insert left-hand needle through both sts from right to left; K2 tog—SSK made.

Instructions

Sock (make 2**)**

Points (make 2 orange and 2 green**)**
Loosely cast on 3 sts.

Row 1:
Inc **(**knit in front and back of next st**)**; knit rem sts—4 sts.

Rows 2 through 5:
Rep Row 1. At end of Row 5—8 sts.

Rows 6 through 11:
Knit.

Cut yarn; slip sts onto stitch holder. Leave last point made on needle.

Ribbing:
Slip points from stitch holders onto needle, alternating colors and having all 32 sts in same direction and yarn ends to right.

Row 12:
With blue, knit.

Divide sts onto 3 needles, having 10 sts on first needle, 12 sts on second needle, and 10 sts on third needle.

Note: Unless otherwise indicated, remainder of sock is worked in rnds.

Rnd 1:
***** K1, P1; rep from ***** around.

Rep Rnd 1 until sock measures 2" **(**2¹/₄"**)** from beg of ribbing.

Turn piece inside out by pushing points through the center of the triangle made by the needles. Yarn strand will be on the left-hand needle. Bring yarn forward, slip one st to right-hand needle; yarn back, slip same st back to left-hand needle.

Next 2 Rnds:
Knit.

Heel:
With green, **(**K4, K2 tog**)** twice; K4. Slip remaining 16 sts onto stitch holder for instep. Turn.

Heel Flap:
Note: Heel flap is worked in rows.

Row 1 (wrong side**):**
Knit.

Rows 2 (right side**) through 17:**
Rep Row 1.

Turning Heel:

Row 1 (right side**):**
K9, K2 tog; K1—11 sts. Turn, leaving rem 2 sts unworked.

Row 2:
Sl 1 as to knit, K5, K2 tog; K1. Turn, leaving rem 2 sts unworked.

Row 3:
Sl 1 as to knit, K6, K2 tog; K1. Turn.

Row 4:
Sl 1 as to knit, K7, K2 tog, K1. Turn, leaving rem st unworked.